Using Scales

Some cooks measure using spoons, but it is more usual to measure using kitchen scales, of which there are many different types.

If you use a tablespoon to measure, one rounded tablespoonful is approximately equal to 25 g (1 ounce).

NOTE For the purposes of this book, 1 pint is approximately 500 millilitres (*ml*), 2 pints one litre, and 1 ounce (*oz*) 25 grams (*g*).

Contents

Acknowledgments

The photographs on pages 1, 23 (bottom), 34, 35, 40, 41, 42, 47 and 48 are by Tim Clark. Cover photograph by John Scott.

Cooking

by LYNNE PEEBLES
photographs by JOHN MOYES

Ladybird Books Loughborough

Scrambled Eggs

A Simple Breakfast

INGREDIENTS	EQUIPMENT
2 eggs	*1 small pan*
25g (1 oz) margarine	*1 wooden spoon*
1 tablespoonful milk	*1 small basin*
1 slice bread and a little butter	*1 fork*
Salt and pepper	*1 tablespoon*
	1 plate

1 Wash your hands and put on an apron.

2 Put plate to warm, butter bread.

3 Gently melt margarine in pan on a low heat. Remove from heat.

4 Add 1 tablespoonful milk.

5 Break each egg in turn into the small basin (to make sure it's fresh) and add to the pan.

6 Add a pinch of salt and a shake of pepper.

7 Stir well. Cook the mixture over a low heat stirring all the time with a wooden spoon.

8 Gradually the eggs will thicken. Scrambled eggs should be soft and creamy. Do not overcook or they will become tough and leathery.

Breakfast is a very important meal and should not be missed. It provides our body with the nutrients to allow it to start its day's work properly. If you do not like a cooked breakfast, then at least begin with a milky drink.

Variations

You can: mix in a little chopped parsley *before* cooking;
stir in 25g (1 oz) grated cheese *after* cooking;
serve on toast or with fried bread;
serve with crispy bacon or fresh tomato.

NOTE Eggs should be stored in a cool place blunt end uppermost.

Separating an Egg

1 Break egg onto saucer.

2 Place an egg cup carefully
over the yolk. Push down
gently.

3 Holding egg cup and saucer
pour off egg white into
bowl, leaving egg yolk
on saucer.

NOTE If egg whites are needed for whisking there
must be no egg yolk broken into them. If this.
happens the egg whites will not whisk up stiffly
but remain soft.

Chocolate Mousse

INGREDIENTS

2 eggs
50g (2 oz) chocolate

EQUIPMENT

1 plate
1 small pan
1 whisk
1 small basin
Mixing bowl
1 tablespoon
2 serving dishes, small

1 Wash your hands and put on an apron.

2 Half fill pan with water and allow to boil. Turn off heat.

3 Break chocolate into pieces, and put in small basin. Place basin over hot water, making sure basin does not touch water.

4 Carefully separate eggs. Place whites in mixing bowl and yolks on a plate.

5 Whisk whites until they stand in firm peaks.

6 Remove basin from pan. Stir egg yolks into chocolate.

7 Add chocolate mixture to egg whites, and fold in very lightly with tablespoon or knife. If mixed too much the mousse will not set.

8 Pour into dishes. Leave in cool place to set.

Chocolate Mousse when set can be decorated with:

a small amount of grated chocolate;
angelica leaves and cherry flowers (a glacé cherry cut
into 8 makes the flowers, with leaves cut from thin
strips of angelica).

Chocolate contains iron which is needed for healthy blood.

Banana Snow

INGREDIENTS

3 bananas
2 egg whites
25 g (1 oz) sugar
A little lemon juice
A few drops of food colouring
Decoration

EQUIPMENT

1 whisk
Mixing bowl
1 small basin
1 fork
Serving dish (or dishes)

1 Wash your hands and put on an apron.

2 Peel the bananas, place in a small basin and mash lightly with a fork, adding a little lemon juice.

3 Place egg whites in mixing bowl, whisk until standing in stiff peaks.

4 Add banana and sugar to egg white and continue whisking until mixture becomes quite stiff.

5 Add a few drops of food colouring, mix well and pour into serving dish or dishes.

6 Decorate with toasted coconut (put a little desiccated coconut on a plate and pop underneath the grill until brown).

NOTE Any fresh fruit when peeled will discolour in the air. Acid in the form of lemon juice will help to prevent this.

Fresh Meat

All meat contains protein and helps our bodies to grow.
Fresh meat should be kept in a cool place and used
within one or two days of purchase. This is because meat
may begin to decay if it is left in a warm room and
harmful food poisoning bacteria may develop.

Preparing Onions

Onions have a strong smell which is released when the
onions are chopped and the onion cells are cut. Your
eyes may water when you prepare onions. To prevent
this, try rinsing onions in cold water after peeling and
before chopping. If your eyes *do* water, don't rub them;
this will only make them worse.

Hints when Frying

Frying means cooking food in hot fat. You can use shallow fat as in a frying pan, or deep fat as in a chip pan.

REMEMBER THE RULE — you *must* have a grown-up with you.

Frying can be dangerous if you are not careful, since any fat used for frying becomes very hot and can burn you badly. Also, any fat spilled onto the cooker may catch fire, then the flames will travel back to the pan and set that on fire. This is dangerous, so you should know what to do.

NEVER put water onto a fat fire

FIRST — turn off the heat

THEN — drape a damp (*not* wet) teatowel over the pan to smother the fire

---

Beefburgers

A Simple Lunch

INGREDIENTS

*200 g (8 oz) fresh minced beef
(will make 4)
1 small onion
30 ml (2 tablespoonfuls)
plain flour
2.5 ml (½ teaspoonful) salt
Few shakes pepper
A little beaten egg
50 g (2 oz) lard
or oil for frying*

EQUIPMENT

*1 frying pan
1 fish slice
1 grater
1 wooden spoon
1 spatula
Measuring spoons*

1 Wash your hands and
  put on an apron.

2 Grate peeled onion into
  mixing bowl, using the
  large cutters of the grater.

3 Put the beef, salt, pepper
  and flour with the onion,
  and mix together.

4 Add enough egg (about 2
  tablespoonfuls) to bind
  the mixture together.

5 Divide the mixture into four. Shape each one to a round on a floured surface.

6 Melt the fat in the pan over a low heat. Use a fish slice to put the beefburgers carefully into the pan.

7 Fry slowly over a low heat for 5 minutes on each side, turning beefburgers carefully with the fish slice and another knife.
If the fat begins to spit, turn down the heat immediately; do not move the pan. Serve with salad or in a bap.

Meatballs in Oxtail Soup

INGREDIENTS

400g (16 oz) minced beef
1 small onion
1 tablespoonful raisins or sultanas
Pinch of salt and pepper
1 medium can of oxtail soup

EQUIPMENT

Ovenproof casserole
Mixing bowl
1 sharp knife
1 plate
1 fork
1 tablespoon
Tin opener

1 Put on oven at Gas Mark 4 (electricity 350°F/180°C).

2 Wash your hands and put on an apron.

3 Top and tail onion, and throw peelings away. Chop with a sharp knife.

4 Place chopped onion in mixing bowl, add meat, sultanas or raisins, and salt and pepper. Mix well together using a fork.

5 Shape into 8 balls (using your hands); put them in bottom of casserole.

6 Pour the soup over the meatballs.

7 Place lid on casserole. Cook in centre of oven for $1\frac{1}{4}$ hours.

8 Serve with potatoes and a green vegetable such as peas.

THAT CASSEROLE IS HOT!
ALWAYS use oven gloves when taking things out of the oven

Scotch Eggs

INGREDIENTS

(*for 4 people*)

4 eggs
200g (8 oz) sausage meat
Brown breadcrumbs
A little milk
A little flour

EQUIPMENT

1 rolling pin
1 baking sheet
Greaseproof paper or foil
2 plates
1 small pan
1 tablespoon
1 fork
Serving dish

1 Put on oven at Gas Mark 5 (electricity 375°F/190°C).

2 Wash your hands and put on an apron.

3 Place eggs in small pan of cold water, bring to the boil and time eggs for 10 minutes.

4 While eggs are boiling, divide sausage meat into 4 pieces, and lightly flour a clean table top. Sprinkle a little flour onto the rolling pin and a little onto the sausage meat. Roll out each piece of sausage meat to the size of a saucer.

5 When eggs are cooked, empty away the hot water, fill pan with cold water and leave eggs to cool for a few minutes.

6 Put breadcrumbs on a plate. Pour a little milk onto the other plate.

7 Take shells off eggs. Rinse in cold water and place one egg in centre of each piece of sausage meat.

8 Wrap sausage meat around each egg and pinch joins gently together.

9 Using a spoon and fork, dip each Scotch egg first into milk then into breadcrumbs.

10 Reshape if necessary on table top.

11 Wrap each Scotch egg in foil or greaseproof paper, and place on baking sheet.

12 Bake for 45 minutes.

13 Serve cut in half lengthways with crisp salad.

17

Rhubarb Crumble

INGREDIENTS		EQUIPMENT
Topping:	*150g (6 oz) plain flour*	*Ovenproof dish*
	75g (3 oz) margarine	*Mixing bowl*
	75g (3 oz) sugar	*1 sieve*
Base:	*400g (16 oz) rhubarb, or fruit*	*1 fork*
	75g (3 oz) sugar	

1 Put on oven at Gas Mark 5 (electricity 375°F/190°C).

2 Wash your hands and put on an apron.

3 Sift flour into mixing bowl, add sugar and margarine. Rub margarine into flour and sugar until there are no large lumps of fat and the mixture looks like fine breadcrumbs.

4 Chop rhubarb and place in dish. Sweeten with 75g (3 oz) sugar.

5 Sprinkle on crumble topping and press down well with a fork. Run fork gently over the top to give a crumbly look.

6 Bake in the centre of the oven for 35 minutes, until just brown.

7 Serve with cream or custard.

Variations

You may use either fresh or tinned fruit to vary this recipe. Baking apples, for example, should be peeled, cut into quarters, then sliced, with 75g (3 oz) sugar to sweeten. If you use tinned fruit, drain off the juice to serve with the crumble along with cream or custard.

Lemon Surprise Pudding

INGREDIENTS

1 packet lemon pie filling
2 eggs
1 small tin pineapple pieces
2 rounded tablespoonfuls sugar
(50g – 2 oz)

EQUIPMENT

1 small pan
1 wooden spoon
1 whisk
Measuring jug
1 metal spoon
2 ovenproof dishes
Mixing bowl
Tin opener

1. Put on oven at Gas Mark 4 (electricity 350°F/180°C).

2. Wash your hands and put on an apron.

3. Open tin of pineapple, place juice in a measuring jug and add water to make up to 250 ml ($\frac{1}{2}$ pint).

4. Separate eggs (see page 6). Place yolks and lemon pie filling in pan; place whites in mixing bowl.

5. Add the 250 ml mixed juice and water to the egg yolks.

6. Place pan on top of cooker and heat gently, stirring all the time, until the lemon mixture comes to the boil and thickens.

7 Add pineapple to lemon sauce, stir well. Pour into the ovenproof dishes.

8 Whisk egg whites until they stand in soft peaks; add 50g (2 oz) sugar and fold in with metal spoon.

9 Spoon mixture on top of lemon sauce in dishes, working from the sides to the centre. Bring mixture up into peaks using the back of a metal spoon.

10 Place dishes in the centre of the oven for 15 minutes until the peaks are golden brown. This pudding can be served hot or cold.

A variation: If liked, a biscuit base may be made to change the pudding into a simple flan.

1 Crush 8 digestive biscuits in a mixing bowl, using the end of a rolling pin.

2 Melt 50g (2 oz) butter gently in a small pan, add to crushed biscuits and mix well. Place biscuit mixture in base of serving dish and press down well. Place lemon mixture on top of biscuit base. Serve cold.

BE SAFE — stay by that pan while butter is melting

21

Cherry and Almond Fingers

INGREDIENTS

Base: 75g *(3 oz) plain flour*
25g *(1 oz) sugar*
50g *(2 oz) margarine*

Middle: 75g *(3 oz) glacé cherries*
25g *(1 oz) sultanas*

Top: 50g *(2 oz) butter*
50g *(2 oz) sugar*
50g *(2 oz) ground almonds*
1 egg

EQUIPMENT

20 cm (8 in)
square cake tin
Mixing bowl
1 wooden spoon
1 knife
1 plate
Greaseproof paper
Serving dish

1 Put on oven at Gas Mark 5 (electricity 375°F/190°C).

2 Wash your hands and put on an apron. Cut greaseproof paper to fit base of tin.

3 Place ingredients for base in mixing bowl, rub fat into flour and sugar with fingertips. Gather dough together and press down well into base of tin.

4 Cut cherries into quarters and sprinkle on top of base with sultanas.

22

5 Place topping ingredients in mixing bowl and mix together with a wooden spoon until smooth and creamy.

6 Spread on top of ingredients in the tin.

7 Bake for 40 minutes in the centre of the oven until firm to touch in centre.

8 Take out of oven and leave to cool in tin. Cut up into sixteen fingers.

DON'T FORGET TO USE OVEN GLOVES!

Coconut Pyramids

INGREDIENTS

75 g (3 oz) desiccated coconut
75 g (3 oz) castor sugar
1 egg white
2 glacé cherries (cut into quarters)

EQUIPMENT

Mixing bowl
1 whisk
1 wooden spoon
1 teaspoon
1 egg cup
Baking sheet (nonstick or greased)

1 Put on oven at Gas Mark 4 (electricity 350°F/180°C).

2 Wash your hands and put on an apron.

3 Place egg white in a mixing bowl. Whisk until white and fluffy.

4 Add sugar and coconut and mix well.

5 Dip egg cup in water and fill with mixture.

6 Shake out gently onto baking sheet. Repeat with rest of mixture.

7 Top each pyramid with a piece of glacé cherry.

8 Bake 15 – 20 minutes until a light golden brown.

Banana Custard

INGREDIENTS

2-3 bananas
500 ml (1 pint) milk
*3 level tablespoonfuls
custard powder*
4 level tablespoonfuls sugar
Decoration

EQUIPMENT

1 pan
1 wooden spoon
1 plate
1 table knife
*1 serving dish or
4 small dishes*

1 Wash your hands and put on an apron.

2 Put custard powder and sugar in pan, add a little of
  the milk and mix to a smooth cream with a wooden
  spoon, gradually adding the rest of the milk.

3 Place on top of the cooker, and heat gently, stirring
  all the time, until the custard mixture begins to
  thicken, then allow to boil for 1 minute, continuing
  to stir all the time.

4 Remove from heat.

5 Peel bananas, cut into
  slices. Add bananas to
  custard, and mix well.
  Pour into serving dish.

This dish may be served
hot or cold. If served cold,
decorate before serving.

Shortbread Biscuits

INGREDIENTS

150g (6oz) plain flour
100g (4oz) butter
50g (2oz) sugar

EQUIPMENT

1 fork
1 pastry knife
1 tablespoon
20cm (8in) cake tin
Greaseproof paper
A little margarine
Mixing bowl

1 Put on oven at Gas Mark 4 (electricity 350°F/180°C).

2 Wash your hands and put on an apron.

3 Cut a circle of greaseproof paper to fit base of tin. Grease inside of tin lightly with margarine, place greaseproof paper in tin.

4 Sift flour into mixing bowl, add sugar and butter.

5 Rub butter into flour and sugar until mixture begins to stick together and then knead to a firm dough.

6 Place dough in cake tin, press out to the sides of the tin with fingers, and flatten with the back of a tablespoon.

7 Mark into portions with a knife and decorate edges. Prick with a fork.

8 Place in centre of oven and bake for 45 minutes until centre of shortbread is firm to the touch.

The oven temperature may be reduced to 300°F/ 150°C or Gas Mark 2 half way through the cooking time to prevent over-browning. The shortbread should be a pale golden colour when cooked.

9 Remove from oven; cut into portions. Turn out of tin when almost cool.

10 A little castor sugar may be sprinkled on top after cooking if desired.

Shortbread may be served with Banana Custard.

Flapjacks

INGREDIENTS

1 full tablespoonful golden syrup (approx. 75g or 3 oz)
75g (3 oz) sugar
75g (3 oz) margarine
150g (6 oz) rolled oats
Pinch of salt
A little lard for greasing

EQUIPMENT

1 18 cm (7 in) cake tin
1 small pan
1 tablespoon
1 teaspoon
1 wooden spoon
Mixing bowl
1 18 cm (7 in) circle greaseproof paper

1 Put on oven at Gas Mark 3 (electricity 325°F/160°C).

2 Wash your hands and put on an apron.

3 Grease inside of tin and line with greaseproof paper.

4 Place golden syrup, margarine and sugar in pan. Put oats and pinch of salt in mixing bowl.

5 Using a wooden spoon, stir ingredients in the pan over a low heat until just melted.

6 Pour into oats and mix well.

7 Put mixture in cake tin and press down, levelling off top as shown below.

8 Place in the oven for 20 minutes until just firm in the centre.

9 Remove from the oven.

10 Mark into portions while still hot.

11 Turn out of tin when cool.

Shortcrust Pastry

INGREDIENTS

200g (8 oz) plain flour
50g (2 oz) lard
50g (2 oz) margarine
Pinch of salt
2½ tablespoonfuls cold water

EQUIPMENT

1 sieve
Mixing bowl
1 table knife
1 tablespoon

When making pastry your hands, the ingredients, and your equipment must all be kept as cool as possible. Start by washing your hands in cold water.

1 Wash your hands and put on an apron.

2 Sift flour and salt into mixing bowl. Add margarine and lard and coat pieces of fat in flour. Cut up margarine and lard into small pieces with a knife.

3 Rub fat into flour, using fingertips, until mixture looks like fine breadcrumbs. (Do not rub fat into flour for too long or the fat will begin to melt and your pastry will be difficult to handle.)

4 Add exactly 2½ tablespoonfuls of cold water to flour mixture and mix in with a knife. Gently gather the mixture together (with your hand) to make a firm dough. The sides of the mixing bowl should be clean and the dough should not be sticky.

5 Leave pastry in a cool place until required. This recipe is the *basic recipe* for shortcrust pastry, and can be used to make many things, such as those on the following pages.

Jam Tarts

INGREDIENTS

Basic recipe for shortcrust pastry
½–¾ jar raspberry jam
A little flour

EQUIPMENT

Rolling pin
2 × 12 bun tins
Pastry cutter
Teaspoon

1 Put on oven at Gas Mark 7 (electricity 425°F/220°C).

2 Make pastry.

3 Sprinkle a little flour onto a clean tabletop and onto your rolling pin.

4 Shape pastry round, using your hands.

5 Roll out pastry lightly using short sharp strokes, moving it on the table top to make sure it is not sticking. Sprinkle on more flour if needed. Roll in one direction only, or pastry may become stretched.

6 Roll out pastry quite thinly.

7 Choose a pastry cutter slightly larger than the top of the bun tins.

8 Cut out circles, as closely together as possible.

9 Pile trimmings, re-roll. You will need 20–24 pastry circles.

10 Place pastry in bun tins, press down slightly.

11 Put a small teaspoonful of jam in the centre of each pastry case. Do not over-fill, or the jam will boil over.

12 Bake towards the top of the oven for 10 minutes, until the pastry is just brown.

13 Remove from bun tins while still hot, and leave to cool.

> SAFETY AGAIN! However delicious they may look, do not eat your jam tarts until they are cool. The jam inside becomes very hot and could easily burn you.

A variation

Follow method for jam tarts up to the end of stage 10, then prick base of each pastry case with a fork. Place in oven without filling and bake for 5-7 minutes until pastry is slightly brown. Remove from oven, put a teaspoonful of lemon curd in each pastry case and allow to cool. (NOTE — Lemon curd is not baked in the pastry as it is a rich mixture containing eggs and cooking may change both flavour and colour.)

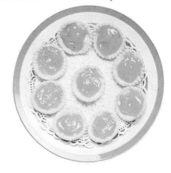

Cheese and Onion Pasties

INGREDIENTS

Basic recipe for shortcrust pastry
100 g (4 oz) Cheddar cheese
1 small onion
A little mashed potato
A few shakes of pepper
A little milk

EQUIPMENT

Rolling pin
1 grater
1 sharp knife
1 plate
1 pastry brush
2 small basins
1 baking sheet
1 small plate or saucer
Mixing bowl

1 Put on oven at Gas Mark 6 (electricity 400°F/200°C).

2 Make pastry. Leave in a cool place.

3 Grate cheese onto plate, then put in mixing bowl.

4 Top, tail, peel and grate onion, add with pepper to cheese and potato and mix well.

5 Sprinkle a little flour onto a clean table top and onto your rolling pin.

6 Shape pastry round, using your hands.
Divide into four.

7 Roll out each piece lightly, using short sharp strokes and rolling in one direction only.

8 Roll out pastry quite thinly.

9 Using a saucer as a guide, cut one circle from each piece.

10 Pile trimmings together, re-roll, and cut out one more circle.

11 Divide cheese and onion mixture into five. Place on each pastry circle.

12 Brush edge of half of each pastry circle with water.

13 Fold one side over and press edges together. Place on baking sheet.

14 Pinch edges to decorate. brush with milk to glaze.

15 Bake 25 – 30 minutes until pastry is golden brown.

DON'T FORGET
THOSE OVEN GLOVES!

Party Pieces

Here are some suggestions for foods you can serve at a party. They are simple to prepare and easy to eat.

Cheese and Pineapple Hedgehog

INGREDIENTS

1 orange
200g (8 oz) Cheddar cheese
Medium can pineapple pieces
Cocktail sticks
1 cherry

EQUIPMENT

1 small flat serving dish
1 small sharp knife

1 Wash your hands and put on an apron.

2 Cut a small slice from one end of the orange.

3 Cut cheese into 1 cm
  ($\frac{1}{2}$ inch) cubes.

4 Spear a piece of pineapple
  and a piece of cheese onto
  each cocktail stick. Push
  into orange.

'Eyes' can be made using two halves of a cherry held
in position with half a cocktail stick.
Pineapple may be changed for small seedless grapes or
halved grapes, or a combination of the two fruits used.

CAREFUL WITH THAT KNIFE — IT'S SHARP!

Sausage Rolls

INGREDIENTS

Basic recipe for shortcrust pastry
or *1 packet frozen puff pastry*
250 g (10 oz) sausage meat
A little milk to glaze

EQUIPMENT

1 rolling pin
1 pastry brush
1 baking sheet
1 small knife

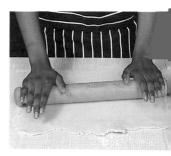

1 Put on oven at Gas Mark 7 (electricity 425°F/220°C).

2 Wash your hands and put on an apron.

3 Lightly sprinkle flour onto a clean table top and onto your rolling pin. If you have made your own pastry, shape it with your hands to an oblong.

4 Roll out the pastry to an oblong approximately 35 cm by 25 cm (14 in by 10 in).

5 Place sausage meat in 2 long rows down length of pastry.

6 Cut pastry down the centre of the two rows of sausage meat. Brush inside edges of the pastry with a little water.

7 Roll pastry over sausage meat from outside, sealing edges together and making sure that joins are underneath.

8 Divide each roll in two, then into four, and if wished into eight.

9 Place on a baking sheet. Brush with milk. Score the top of each sausage roll with a knife or snip with scissors.

10 Bake for 15 – 20 minutes until sausage rolls are a golden brown colour. Remove from baking sheet to cool.

NOTE For easy cleaning leave baking sheet to soak in water before washing.

Vanilla Icecream

INGREDIENTS

2 eggs
50 g (2 oz) icing sugar
¼ teaspoonful vanilla essence
1 packet Bird's Dream Topping
125 ml (¼ pint) milk

EQUIPMENT

Mixing bowl
2 small basins
1 whisk
1 tablespoon
1 teaspoon
1 plastic container or
ice tray

Set refrigerator to its coldest setting, and choose a container for your icecream that will fit into the icebox of your fridge.

1 Wash your hands and put on an apron.

2 Empty Dream Topping into a mixing bowl and whisk with 125 ml milk until smooth.

3 Separate eggs. Put yolks in one small basin, and put whites in the other small basin.

4 Add half the icing sugar to the egg yolks with
¼ teaspoonful vanilla essence and mix well.

5 Whisk egg whites until standing in soft peaks, whisk
in remaining icing sugar.

6 Add yolk mixture, and egg whites, to the Dream
Topping and whisk well. Pour into freezing container.

7 Freeze for at least two hours until firm.

Flavoured Icecream

Instead of using vanilla essence, you could try:

Rum and raisin (¼ teaspoonful rum essence,
25 – 50 g (1 – 2 oz) raisins).

Strawberry or raspberry (in summer 100 g (4 oz) of
fresh fruit can be whisked into the Dream Topping.
When not available, substitute two tablespoonfuls of
milk shake syrup).

Chocolate (make vanilla icecream first, then add
grated or chopped chocolate together with a little
cocoa or drinking chocolate if desired).

Banana Split

INGREDIENTS

For each split:
1 banana
A few nuts or a little grated chocolate
A little fruit syrup
A scoop of icecream
A little whipped cream

EQUIPMENT

1 knife
1 small serving dish

1 Wash your hands and put on an apron.

2 Peel banana, and slice lengthways. Place slices on dish with a space between them.

3 Place a scoop of icecream in the centre, and a rosette of whipped cream.

4 Pour on a little fruit syrup, sprinkle with nuts or chocolate and serve immediately.

Peach Melba

INGREDIENTS

*1 medium can peach halves
or slices*
A little strawberry syrup
A few split almonds
4 – 6 cherries
4 – 6 scoops icecream
8 – 12 icecream wafers

EQUIPMENT

4 – 6 serving dishes
Tin opener

1 Wash your hands and put on an apron.

2 Place half a peach in each dish, cut side uppermost.
Top each with a scoop of icecream.

3 Pour on a little syrup. Use split almonds to make
leaves, place cherry in centre to make flower.

4 Add wafers and serve immediately.

Cheese Baked Potatoes

INGREDIENTS

(8 portions)

4 medium-sized old potatoes
100g (4 oz) grated Cheddar cheese
50g (2 oz) butter or margarine
1 tablespoonful milk
1 sliced tomato
Salt and pepper

EQUIPMENT

1 baking sheet
1 fork
1 teaspoon
1 small sharp knife
1 grater
1 plate
1 basin
Flat serving dish
8 paper napkins

1 Put on oven at Gas Mark 6 (electricity 400°F/200°C).

2 Wash your hands and put on an apron.

3 Scrub potatoes well in plenty of cold water. Prick each one with a fork 6 times. Put onto baking sheet.

4 Place in oven for approximately 1 hour until cooked. (*To test:* Push the point of knife into the centre of the potato; the knife should slide in and out easily when potato is cooked.)

5 When potatoes are cooked, cut in half lengthways. Scoop out centre with a teaspoon, then put in basin.

6 Add milk, margarine, salt and pepper and three-quarters of the grated cheese. Mix well.

7 Pile potato mixture back into potato shells. Sprinkle remaining cheese on top.

8 Return potatoes to the oven for 15–20 minutes until cheese melts and browns.

9 Top each potato with a slice of tomato.

10 Place each potato on a paper napkin and then onto serving dish.

Variations

Chopped parsley or ham may also be added when potato mixture is mixed together.

REMEMBER — bend your knees and not your back when putting things into and taking them out of the oven

---

45

Open Rolls

Instead of making sandwiches, try open rolls; they are as delicious to eat as they are to look at. When shopping, choose long finger rolls or round rolls.

1 Wash your hands and put on an apron.

2 Cut rolls in half and spread each cut side with butter.

3 *Toppings:* Choose one or more foods from each column and arrange food attractively on top of rolls:

Sliced ham	Cress	Raisins
Corned beef	Lettuce	Halved grapes
Cheese sliced or grated	Cucumber	Orange slices
Hard-boiled egg	Sliced tomato	Pineapple
Salmon or tuna mixed with a little mayonnaise	Tomato wedges	

*Make them look
interesting!*

How about:
Lettuce and ham on a cocktail stick?
A slice of orange for a sail?
Lettuce with sliced cheese sail, and grape on top of mast?
Scrambled egg and cress with orange wings?
Salmon and mayonnaise with cucumber wings?

Party Drinks — *Colourful drinks to help the party spirit!*

Orange and Lemon Fizz

INGREDIENTS
makes 1 litre (2 pints)
1 lemon
250 ml (½ pint) orange squash
1 bottle lemonade
Ice cubes

EQUIPMENT
Lemon squeezer
Small sharp knife
Jug
Glasses

1 Wash your hands and put on an apron.

2 Cut lemon in half and cut one half into 3–4 slices. Squeeze juice from other half, place in jug.

3 Add orange squash and ice cubes. Pour on lemonade.

4 Float lemon slices on top and serve.

Strawberry Marshmallow Float

INGREDIENTS

1 carton strawberry yogurt
500 ml (1 pint) cold milk
6 marshmallows

EQUIPMENT

1 whisk
Mixing bowl
3 glasses

1 Whisk milk and yogurt together until frothy.

2 Pour into glasses, float marshmallows on top.

3 Chill and serve.

To frost glasses

When cold drinks are served at a party, the glasses can be made to look more attractive if they are frosted.

INGREDIENTS

1 egg white
A little castor sugar

EQUIPMENT

1 whisk
Mixing bowl
Glasses

1 Wash your hands and put on an apron.

2 Lightly whisk egg white until just frothy.

3 Dip glass upside down in egg white so that 1 cm ($\frac{1}{2}$ in) of rim only is moistened.

4 Dip in sugar, then allow to dry in warm room.

5 Glasses must be filled carefully when serving.

Now you can make all the things in this book, why not ask your friends to a party?

51

Index